THE POETRY OF HAFNIUM

The Poetry of Hafnium

Walter the Educator

Silent King Books - SKB

Copyright © 2024 by Walter the Educator

All rights reserved. No part of this book may be reproduced in any manner whatsoever without written permission except in the case of brief quotations embodied in critical articles and reviews.

First Printing, 2024

Disclaimer
This book is a literary work; poems are not about specific persons, locations, situations, and/or circumstances unless mentioned in a historical context. This book is for entertainment and informational purposes only. The author and publisher offer this information without warranties expressed or implied. No matter the grounds, neither the author nor the publisher will be accountable for any losses, injuries, or other damages caused by the reader's use of this book. The use of this book acknowledges an understanding and acceptance of this disclaimer.

dedicated to all the chemistry lovers in the world, like myself

HAFNIUM

In the heart of the periodic table's domain,

HAFNIUM

Lies a metal of glory, Hafnium its name.

HAFNIUM

With atomic number seventy-two it claims,

HAFNIUM

A story of elements, each with its aims.

HAFNIUM

In the cosmos, it dwells, amid stars and space,

HAFNIUM

A shimmering beacon, in the celestial race.

HAFNIUM

Born from the furnace of a stellar embrace,

HAFNIUM

Its essence imbued with a heavenly grace.

HAFNIUM

A titan among metals, noble and strong,

HAFNIUM

In the annals of chemistry, it does belong.

HAFNIUM

With electrons that dance to a cosmic song,

HAFNIUM

Hafnium's allure, forever lifelong.

HAFNIUM

Its lustrous allure, a captivating sight,

HAFNIUM

In the laboratory's glow, it shines so bright.

HAFNIUM

A testament to science, its profound might,

HAFNIUM

Unlocking mysteries, in the dead of night.

HAFNIUM

From zirconium it springs, a close kin,

HAFNIUM

Separated by methods, ingenious within.

HAFNIUM

With properties unique, it does begin,

HAFNIUM

A journey of discovery, under the din.

HAFNIUM

In alloys it plays, a crucial role,

HAFNIUM

Enhancing materials, achieving the goal.

HAFNIUM

In turbines it spins, with grace and control,

HAFNIUM

Pushing boundaries, to reach the highest pole.

HAFNIUM

But beyond its utility, lies a tale,

HAFNIUM

Of atoms and bonds, in a cosmic sail.

HAFNIUM

From stars to Earth, it does prevail,

HAFNIUM

A journey of wonder, without fail.

HAFNIUM

In nuclear reactors, it finds its home,

HAFNIUM

A realm of energy, where atoms roam.

HAFNIUM

Capturing neutrons, in a fertile loam,

HAFNIUM

Powering civilizations, to kingdoms dome.

HAFNIUM

Yet in the realm of art, it finds its voice,

HAFNIUM

In hues of ceramics, it does rejoice.

HAFNIUM

A palette of colors, to freely deploy,

HAFNIUM

In artisans' hands, a masterpiece to employ.

HAFNIUM

From Earth's crust to the laboratory's sight,

HAFNIUM

Hafnium's journey, a beacon of light.

HAFNIUM

In the tapestry of elements, it takes flight,

HAFNIUM

A testament to nature's wondrous might.

HAFNIUM

So let us marvel at Hafnium's grace,

HAFNIUM

In the symphony of atoms, in every space.

HAFNIUM

A bridge between worlds, in the cosmic race,

HAFNIUM

Hafnium, a marvel, in the universe's embrace.

HAFNIUM

ABOUT THE CREATOR

Walter the Educator is one of the pseudonyms for Walter Anderson. Formally educated in Chemistry, Business, and Education, he is an educator, an author, a diverse entrepreneur, and he is the son of a disabled war veteran. "Walter the Educator" shares his time between educating and creating. He holds interests and owns several creative projects that entertain, enlighten, enhance, and educate, hoping to inspire and motivate you.

Follow, find new works, and stay up to date
with Walter the Educator™
at WaltertheEducator.com

www.ingramcontent.com/pod-product-compliance
Lightning Source LLC
LaVergne TN
LVHW020134080526
838201LV00119B/3865